THE LAST DAYS OF STEAM
ON THE
LONDON MIDLAND
REGION

Heavy goods trains required the assistance of a banker on the long drag up Shap. No. 48136 is pictured going well, the driver taking the opportunity to look round. This engine was completed at Crewe works in August 1941 and withdrawn in March 1967.

9.63

THE LAST DAYS OF STEAM
ON THE
LONDON MIDLAND
REGION

– ERIC SAWFORD –

SUTTON PUBLISHING

First published in the United Kingdom in 2000
Sutton Publishing Ltd · Phoenix Mill · Thrupp · Stroud · Gloucestershire · GL5 2BU

British Library Cataloguing-in-Publication Data
A catalogue record for this book is available from the British Library.

ISBN 0-7509-0413-5

Title page photograph: 'Black Five' no. 44927 had arrived at Low Moor shed with a special and is pictured here ready to turn on the turntable. This depot was originally owned by the Lancashire & Yorkshire Railway and had Class 5s allocated to it throughout the 1950s.

13.5.56

Typeset in 9/10 Palatino.
Typesetting and origination by
Sutton Publishing Limited.
Printed in Great Britain by
Butler & Tanner, Frome, Somerset.

Introduction

Sir William Stanier was appointed Chief Mechanical Engineer of the LMS in 1932 and it was not long before the first of his designs appeared. During his twelve-year term of office he introduced a number of new classes, which meant that a large proportion of the engines that became London Midland Region stock in 1948 were of modern design. There were, of course, numerous engines still in service that had been introduced by previous Chief Mechanical Engineers. Some of these, including the last remaining passenger locomotives of the London & North Western Railway, were to quickly disappear. The west coast main line passenger services remained firmly in the hands of Staniers, 'Princess Royal' and 'Coronation' classes on the heaviest trains, together with the 'Royal Scots' introduced by Sir Henry Fowler. The Jubilee class 4–6–0s were also used and handled the principal trains on the former Midland main line. The Midland 4–4–0 'Compounds' fared much better than the LNWR passenger engines, the last of these being withdrawn soon after Nationalisation. In their final days the Midland 'Compounds' were relegated to secondary services.

The introduction in 1934 of W. Stanier's famous Class 5 mixed traffic 4–6–0s resulted in many older engines making their final journeys. 'Black Fives' – as they were (and still are) referred to – were capable of handling heavy expresses. They were also used on numerous other duties, and they were some of the last steam locomotives to work on British Railways in normal service. In total, 580 'Black Fives' were built, and some were even produced after Nationalisation, a number of them experimental versions. The first of these appeared in 1947 with external Stephenson link motion, Timken roller bearings and a double chimney. Over the next four years engines with Caprotti valve gear and other variations were introduced.

The first batch of Standard Class 5s were built at Derby works. No. 73006 was undergoing steaming and running trials when this picture was taken.

2.7.51

Royal Scot class no. 46123 *Royal Irish Fusilier* of Edge Hill (Liverpool) depot stands at Rugby, heading 'The Manxman'. The locomotive was running without windshields at this time.

3.7.51

The principal heavy goods locomotives of the LNWR were 0–8–0s, while the Midland Railway relied on smaller engines, double-heading if necessary, with a huge number in service. The introduction of the Beyer-Garratt 2–6–6–2Ts and Stanier 8Fs on the heavy coal trains released many of the 0–6–0s for lighter duties. The need for a Standard heavy goods engine soon became apparent, and as a result in 1935 Stanier introduced his very successful taper boiler 8F 2–8–0 design; well over six hundred were eventually to be found in service. The veteran LNWR 0–8–0s were slowly reduced in number, although examples of these very useful engines survived through to the last decade of steam on British Railways. In their final years these locomotives, with their very distinctive whistling and wheezing sounds, were mostly used on lighter trains.

The London Midland Region inherited a large number of 0–6–0T shunting locomotives. By far the most numerous were the 3Fs, commonly known as 'Jinties'. These were a post-Grouping development of an earlier Midland Railway design, and there were over four hundred in service. You could not travel far before you came across a 'Jinty': most sheds had at least one in their allocation. Depots with large shunting yards nearby typically had a stud of these very useful engines.

Tank locomotives of 2–6–2 and 2–6–4 designs were one of the mainstays of local passenger services. The LMR operated a considerable number of 2–6–4s, of Fowler, Stanier and Fairburn designs. The latter were a development of the Stanier engines introduced in 1945 but with a shorter wheelbase and detail alterations. The 2–6–2Ts were also of Fowler and Stanier designs, introduced in 1930 and 1935 respectively. In 1946 the first of the H.G. Ivatt lightweight 2MT 2–6–0s appeared, together with a 2–6–2 tank version. The introduction of these two classes resulted in the withdrawal of many pre-Grouping engines which had survived on branch and cross-country services where weight restrictions ruled out the use of heavier locomotives. The first of the tender

The siding at the back of Wellingborough shed was frequently used to store surplus locomotives for long periods. 3P no. 41966 stood there for a considerable time, still with British Railways lettering on the tank side and the front number just painted on.

5.7.51

During the early 1950s the Beyer-Garratts were a familiar sight hauling heavy coal trains on the Midland main line. The revolving coal bunker fitted to all but two of the class can be clearly seen in this picture of no. 47988, taken at Wellingborough.

5.7.51

'Jubilee' no. 45666 *Cornwallis* stands at Llandudno Junction, heading a special on its way to the seaside resort at Llandudno.

30.6.51

engines were sent to Kettering depot to replace veteran ex-Midland 0–6–0s on the Cambridge services via Huntingdon East. These modern locomotives with their comfortable cabs were immediately welcomed by the enginemen who had put up with the spartan conditions on the 0–6–0s for years. It was not long before the first of the ex-Midland engines was put into store. Eventually the Cambridge services were entirely worked by the 2MTs, although in the final years these were joined by two Standard 2MTs, nos 78020/1. The Ivatt designs, both tender and tank, were to prove themselves very capable and were used as the basis for the 78xxx and 84xxx Standard locomotives.

The Midland Railway's small engine policy, the numbers of engines considerably increased by the LMS, resulted in a large number of 0–6–0s being handed over to British Railways in 1948. Among them was the 4F design which had been added to by a 1924 post-Grouping development of well over five hundred engines. The principal passenger locomotives of the Midland Railway were 4–4–0s; here again in LMS days a considerable number of 'Compounds' were built. Exactly the same thing happened with the smaller 2P 4–4–0s; a post-Grouping development was introduced in 1928 with modified dimensions and reduced boiler mountings. The smaller 4–4–0s were principally used on secondary services and also as pilots on express trains.

In 1929 Fowler introduced an 0–8–0 design developed from the very useful G2A class, although they were never as good as the G2As. The 0–8–0s that became London Midland Region stock were all located in the north of England and became extinct long before the last examples of the LNWR design were withdrawn.

Another company which became part of the LMS at Grouping was the Lancashire & Yorkshire. The L&Y engines which transferred into LMR stock were principally 3F 0–6–0s, some of which moved to depots a long way from their home territory; several were even to be found at sheds in North Wales. The earlier 2F design by Barton Wright still had a few survivors. Another class represented by a considerable number of engines was the 0–6–0ST; these were rebuilds of an early 0–6–0 tender design and became the standard L&Y shunting locomotives.

By the mid-1950s work was becoming scarce for many of the small pre-Grouping tank engines, including the L&Y 2–4–2Ts, a number of their duties having been taken over by more modern designs. At this time some examples went into store, while others were transferred to depots well away from their former haunts. Wellingborough received some for local branch working, although it was not long before modern engines replaced them. The remaining ex-LNWR 2–4–2Ts of power classification 1P, with their distinctive tall chimneys, were also soon to disappear; these and the 0–6–2Ts, known as 'Coal Tanks', shared the distinction of being the last LNWR small tanks in normal service on British Railways. The last survivors of the two LNWR 0–6–0 tender designs – known as 'Coal Engines' and 'Cauliflowers' – were rapidly reduced in number after Nationalisation, although several of these veteran engines survived for a short time in service stock where they were built. Crewe works also had a 'Special Tank', no. 3323, still carrying its LNWR number, and the last two remaining Bissel truck design 0–4–02STs. Wolverton carriage works had four of the 'Special Tanks', introduced in 1870; these travelled the short distance to Bletchley depot for any repairs.

Every railway where there were tight curves had a requirement for short-wheelbase tank locomotives for shunting work. Many of these were saddle tanks, and among them were small engines of Midland Railway origin, plus ten side tanks introduced by Deeley in 1907. There were also a number of more modern small saddle tanks. First introduced in 1932, these were a Kitson design with modifications as required by W. Stanier, Chief Mechanical Engineer at the time.

One of Stanier's first designs after taking office was a small class of ten 0–4–4Ts, push-and-pull fitted for branch line work. Numbered 41900–09, these seldom received much attention, and two were to be found at Watford for several years. The last few remaining ex-Midland 0–4–4Ts mostly ended their days on shed pilot duties.

An early morning train bound for Chester awaits the right away from Llandudno station, headed by 5MT 2–6–0 no. 42975. These locomotives were occasionally seen on passenger services.

30.6.51

The ex-LNWR 0–6–2Ts, known as 'Coal Tanks', were noted for their sharp exhaust. No. 58908 spent some time at Bletchley as shed pilot. I was lucky to catch the engine standing in splendid isolation – it was just four months away from withdrawal.

6.8.51

One famous locomotive, sadly cut up at the end of its long service, was the Lickey banker 0–10–0 no. 58100, often referred to as 'Big Bertha'. This engine was allocated to Bromsgrove and was used to bank both passenger and goods trains on the famous Lickey incline. It made occasional visits to Derby works but remained at Bromsgrove for many years until withdrawal. With its 43,315lb tractive effort it made a splendid sight as it blasted up the bank.

Another very useful class of mixed traffic locomotives was introduced in 1926. The 2–6–0 5MTs were widely known as 'Crabs' owing to the unmistakable outline of their large inclined cylinders. They were to be found at many LMS depots, with all 245 examples later becoming London Midland Region stock. These locomotives had 5ft 6in driving wheels and a tractive effort greater than the 'Black Fives', and were capable of a fair turn of speed when required. They were normally used on fast goods and parcels, but during the summer months they were often seen on excursions and specials. Like the 'Crabs', the un-rebuilt 'Patriots' were also easily recognisable and filled a similar role, although they were used more often on parcels and secondary passenger services than on fast goods. It was a different story with the rebuilt engines introduced by Ivatt in 1946; these were purely express locomotives, the rebuilding upgrading them to a 7P power classification.

There was also another useful class of forty 5MTs which quietly went about their business. These were a taper boiler Stanier 2–6–0 design introduced in 1933. During the 1950s some depots used them on secondary passenger work, but by the mid-1950s they were mostly used on goods working and were largely overshadowed by the well-known Class 5s. The lightweight Ivatt 2–6–0s introduced in 1946 principally for branch line working attracted considerable attention, but in the following year even more comments were passed about another Ivatt 2–6–0 design. These had a high running plate and the

The first Ivatt 4MT 2–6–0s were fitted with huge double chimneys when they entered service, and this caused much comment at the time. These double chimneys did not last for long before they were replaced by a more conventional pattern. This is no. 43019, pictured at Nottingham.

6.7.51

first examples had a massive double chimney; the later engines had more conventional chimneys, which were subsequently fitted on to the early examples. The Ivatt 4MT was another excellent design with construction going on well into BR days. These engines were also used as the basis for the Standard 4MT 2–6–0s which were modified with BR standard fittings. Their early duties included the Bletchley–Cambridge services. Eventually the Ivatts were also to be found at many depots other than those in the London Midland Region and examples of the class remained in service almost to the end of steam on British Railways. Only one has survived into preservation.

The LMS operated over a huge area of England and also extensively on the western side of Scotland. It had services to, and depots in, Edinburgh, Dundee and Aberdeen. This was to change with the formation of British Railways in 1948 when the Scottish Region was formed. The London Midland Region consisted of twenty-four districts in the mid-1950s, which extended as far north as Carlisle. A considerable number of depots had allocations around the one hundred mark; surprisingly none exceeded two hundred, with Saltley being the nearest with 191 in 1954. There were, of course, changes to the allocations over the following years as engines were transferred to other regions. Two districts covered the London area. The west coast main line came under Willesden (1A), with an allocation of 143 locomotives. (This did not include the top link passenger engines, which were to be found at Camden (1B). The Midland main line came under Cricklewood (14A), but again the express engines were to be found at the second shed, Kentish Town (14B). During the 1950s the heavy expresses to and from St Pancras were principally worked by Jubilee class 4–6–0s and the 'maids of all work' Stanier Class 5s.

The area covered by the London Midland Region was vast and included Birmingham, Manchester, Nottingham, Liverpool, Sheffield, Carlisle and Bristol, with countless small towns also served. There were a number of depots in and around Birmingham and Manchester. The average allocation for many London Midland Region sheds was around forty–fifty; some were much larger, while others had as few as just eight locomotives.

The pictures chosen for this book range from the early 1950s through to the end of steam on British Railways in 1968. The London Midland Region had the distinction of being the last to operate steam in regular service, although by that time such engines were confined to a small area around Liverpool, Preston and Manchester. The locomotives to be seen in the 1950s included many pre-Grouping examples, in the case of some classes in very small numbers. The introduction of the Standard designs and ever-increasing numbers of diesels decimated the ranks of the older engines. Shunting yards, once the domain of 'Jinties' and other small steam locomotives, were taken over by diesel shunters. By the mid-1950s older engines were frequently to be seen stored at many depots, some with the traditional piece of tarpaulin tied over the chimney and with the motion greased. Others were simply dumped at the end of a siding. Many of the older classes all too soon became extinct with the ex-LNWR engines faring especially badly; the one exception was the 0–8–0s, although inroads were slowly being made in their numbers too. By the end of this period classes had been considerably reduced, with line closures and diesel multiple units making even more engines surplus to requirements.

Early in the 1950s the standard of cleanliness was still quite high, though it did vary from depot to depot. Passenger locomotives were generally smart in external appearance and in good mechanical condition. By the 1960s it was very different. Goods engines returned from general overhaul resplendent in a shiny coat of black paint, but after just a few weeks without regular attention they were as grubby as the rest. Early in the 1960s steam began to be eliminated from some areas, and as a result the numbers of engine withdrawals increased rapidly. Until this time unwanted engines were cut up at locomotive works, but such were the numbers now being withdrawn that engines were sold on to private scrapyards and the sad sight of these locomotives being towed away for scrap became common. They often faced quite lengthy journeys: Cohens near Kettering, for example, received engines from London Midland, as well as some from the Southern, Western and Eastern Regions.

By the mid-1960s a number of the named engines in service had lost their nameplates and, in many cases, their front numberplates, too. The general condition of most still in service was deplorable as depots just could not wait to change over to diesel power. As steam was phased out so the numbers of enthusiast specials increased, and this resulted in some locomotives regaining something of their former glory, albeit for a short time. The remaining steam depots in 1967 and 1968 became Meccas for enthusiasts, many of whom were convinced that when steam finished they would never see it again on main lines. The final fling of steam in the north is well known, and the last trains caused unprecedented traffic jams on some roads as enthusiasts flocked in their thousands to witness the final steam specials.

Fortunately, a considerable number of London Midland Region locomotives have survived into preservation. Some have been carefully restored and are in full working order, while others, after years of exposure to the elements, still remain very much in the condition in which they were rescued. Sadly, the massive costs of restoration to working order make it doubtful if they will ever work again.

The pictures chosen for this book have been selected to illustrate as many types as possible within an eighteen-year period, right up to the end of steam. They show that the London Midland Region had plenty more than just the well-known 'Black Fives' and 'Eight Freights', although these important classes have certainly not been overlooked.

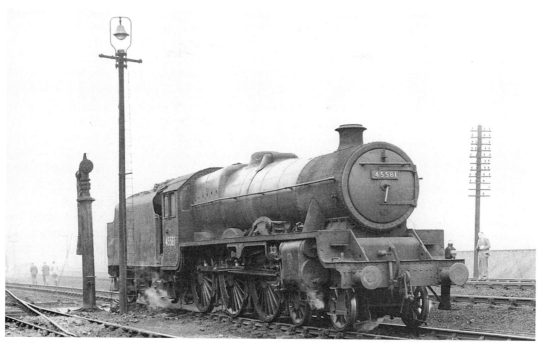

'Jubilee' class no. 45581 *Bihar and Orissa* draws up to the water crane at its home depot, Farnley Junction. This locomotive was one of the sizable batch constructed by the North British Locomotive Company. Completed in October 1934, it was condemned in August 1966.

24.6.56

Most London Midland Region depots had at least one 'Jinty' in their allocation, while those close to large marshalling yards had many more. During the mid-1950s Camden had thirteen 'Jinties' which were mostly used on stock workings; this is no. 47667 ready for its next turn of duty.

20.3.55

Five members of the 'Princess Royal' class were allocated to Edge Hill (Liverpool) depot, including no. 46204 *Princess Louise*, seen here coming on shed at Camden after working in with an express from Liverpool. It is about to pass one of the depot's 'Jinties' awaiting its next duty.

20.3.55

No. 46204 *Princess Louise* under the coaling tower at Camden. Note the visitors deep in conversation. The 'Princess Royals' were the first of the Stanier Pacifics and appeared five years before his famous 'Coronation' class, which had a slightly higher tractive effort.

20.3.55

Class 8F 2–8–0 no. 48549 starts the climb to cross the east coast main line at Sandy on its way to Bletchley. During the 1950s many heavy goods trains worked over this route, which was a good east–west connection. Currently plans are afoot to restore such a service.

31.7.54

Several members of the 'Patriot' class ran nameless for their entire working lives, and no. 45517 was one of them. Seen here leaving Camden shed, no. 45517 was a Willesden engine. In the mid-1950s both these depots had 'Patriots' in their allocation, which were often seen on parcels and fast goods workings.

13.11.55

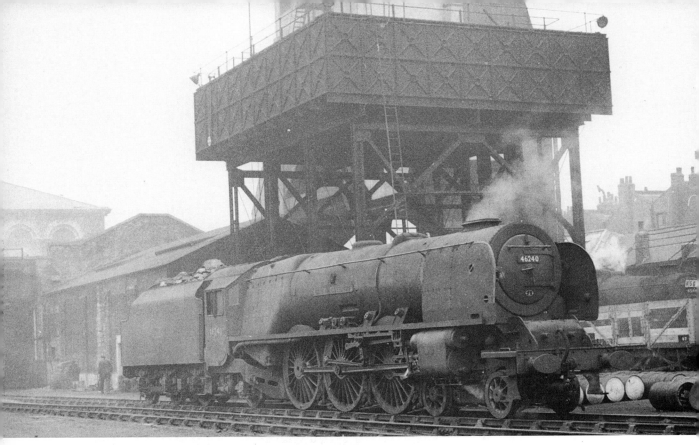

I visited Camden shed several times but I was never lucky enough to have bright clear conditions. Always a cloud of smoke hung over the depot, as was the case when this picture of no. 46240 *City of Coventry* was taken. This locomotive was one of fifteen allocated to Camden.

13.11.55

Sandy station, with 4MT 2–6–4T no. 80083 ready to depart for Cambridge heading a typical four-coach train with a horsebox next to the locomotive. The signal box just visible on the left controlled the Cambridge line only.

31.7.54

Ex-L&Y 0–6–0 no. 52619, seen here at Rhyl shed, was one of the Class 27 rebuilds. These were superheated, with a higher boiler pressure and piston valves. Several depots on the North Wales coast line had these engines in their allocation.

10.8.52

Every so often railway enthusiasts had a lucky break, and this was the case when I visited Rugby depot to find a work-stained ex-LNWR 1P 2–4–2T, no. 46654, under repair and standing in the yard. All too often veterans such as this would be left out of use at the back of the shed. No. 46654 was already running out of time – it had just seven more months in service.

5.2.53

During the 1950s many of these veteran ex-LNWR 0–8–0s remained in service. No. 49245 is seen here coaling at Coventry depot. These locomotives never carried front number plates. Coventry (shedcode 2D) and Warwick were the smallest sheds in the Rugby district, with just twelve locomotives each; five of the Coventry engines were ex-LNWR 0–8–0s.

5.12.53

In the smoky atmosphere of Camden depot 'Royal Scot' no. 46170 *British Legion* stands coaled and watered ready for its next duty. At the time Camden was home to twelve 'Royal Scots' including *Royal Scot* itself. *British Legion,* was rebuilt from the high pressure experimental engine no. 6399 *Fury.*

20.3.55

Standard locomotives replaced many veterans on cross-country and branch services. Here a Standard Class 4 4–6–0, no. 75034, approaches Sandy with a Cambridge to Bletchley service. This line was originally part of the LNWR system. All that remains is a section from Bedford to Bletchley.

31.7.54.

A considerable number of ex-Midland Railway 2P class 4–4–0s ended their days on cross-country services, and the lightly loaded trains were well within their capabilities. No. 40526 of Burton depot, seen here at Walton, heads a Peterborough to Leicester service.

4.8.54

(*Opposite top*) In the early 1950s a small number of these ex-Midland 1F 0–6–0Ts remained in the allocation of Kentish Town MPD. some were 'half cabs', such as no. 41724 pictured here. This class was introduced in 1878, and many were later rebuilt with Belpaire boilers. No. 41724 was rebuilt, although it did not receive a new all-over cab.

20.3.55

(*Opposite bottom*) Two 'Jubilees' await their next turn of duty in one of the roundhouses of Kentish Town depot. On the left is no. 45683 *Hogue*, a visitor from Millhouses; on the right is no. 45557 *New Brunswick*, a Kentish Town engine. 'Jubilees' were the principal express locomotives on the Midland main line at this time and *New Brunswick* was one of several allocated to Kentish Town.

20.3.55

Standard class 4MT no. 80082 stands in the south end bay platform at Cambridge ready to depart with a Bletchley train via Sandy. The 4MT was in a grubby state but someone has cleaned the number on the bunker side. Note the horsebox next to the engine: they were a familiar sight on these trains.

9.5.55

This 3F 0–6–0T no. 47214 was one of the members of the class rebuilt with Belpaire boilers and condensing equipment for use in the London area. The famous 'Jinties' were a post-Grouping development of this design with detail alterations. Another member of the class can be seen in the background.

20.3.55

Kentish Town depot was responsible for passenger workings out of St Pancras. In the mid-1950s it had an allocation of one hundred locomotives, nearly twenty more than the principal shed of the district, Cricklewood. Class 5 no. 44944 was a visitor from Sheffield.

20.3.55

'Jubilee' class locomotives were a common sight on the west coast main line. Here no. 45740 *Munster* heads a northbound express on the long climb out of Euston. At this time it was a Camden locomotive, one of the ten 'Jubilees' allocated to that depot.

20.3.55

'Royal Scot' class no. 46170 *British Legion* at Camden shed. Rebuilt in 1935 from the experimental high pressure engine no. 6399 *Fury*, no. 46170 was a Camden engine during the mid-1950s.

20.3.55

(*Opposite top*) Photographed in the murky depths of Bradford Manningham depot, this is 4F no. 44400 awaiting its next duty. These very useful locomotives were allocated to many London Midland Region depots.

13.5.56

(*Opposite bottom*) The driver of 3F 0–6–0 no. 43183 checks round his engine before leaving Normanton depot. This locomotive was an example of those fitted with 4ft 11in driving wheels. The 3Fs were particularly useful for pick-up and local freight trains.

13.5.56

'Royal Scot' class no. 46136 *The Border Regiment* pictured climbing Camden bank with a Holyhead express. The locomotive's crew are taking the opportunity to look at what was happening on Camden shed as they pass by.

20.3.55

The numerous 0–6–0 designs were 'maids of all work' during the 1950s. A considerable number of ex-L&Y 0–6–0 locomotives were still active: this is no. 52343 in typical work-stained condition at Low Moor depot.

13.5.56

The introduction of the useful Ivatt 2–6–2T resulted in many veterans making their final journey. These engines were the tank version of the lightweight 2MT 2–6–0 design, and were ideal for branch line services. They were warmly welcomed by the enginemen not least for their comfortable cabs. No. 41247 is seen here at Bradford Manningham.

13.5.56

Photography in some sheds was only possible by standing on the turntable; this was the case when I took this picture of 3F 0–6–0s nos 43553 and 43784 at Bradford Manningham, originally a Midland Railway depot. Roundhouses were ideal for number collectors as they could list everything very quickly and be ready for off, but this left photographers very little time!

13.5.56

Ivatt 2MT no. 46449 heads south through Rugby station with steam escaping from numerous places. It is not known why it was in the area but it was certainly a long way from home, being allocated to Penrith at the time.

5.2.53

(*Opposite top*) The Johnson 'half cab' 0–6–0Ts were introduced in 1878 by the Midland Railway; those that still survived in the 1950s were mostly to be found as shed pilots and on local shunting work. No. 41661 was the Stourton depot pilot.

13.5.56

(*Opposite bottom*) Jubilee' class no. 45613 *Kenya* awaits its next turn of duty at Camden depot. This engine was fitted with a high-sided tender. 'Jubilees' were a common sight on the west coast main line, especially on the Birmingham trains.

13.11.55

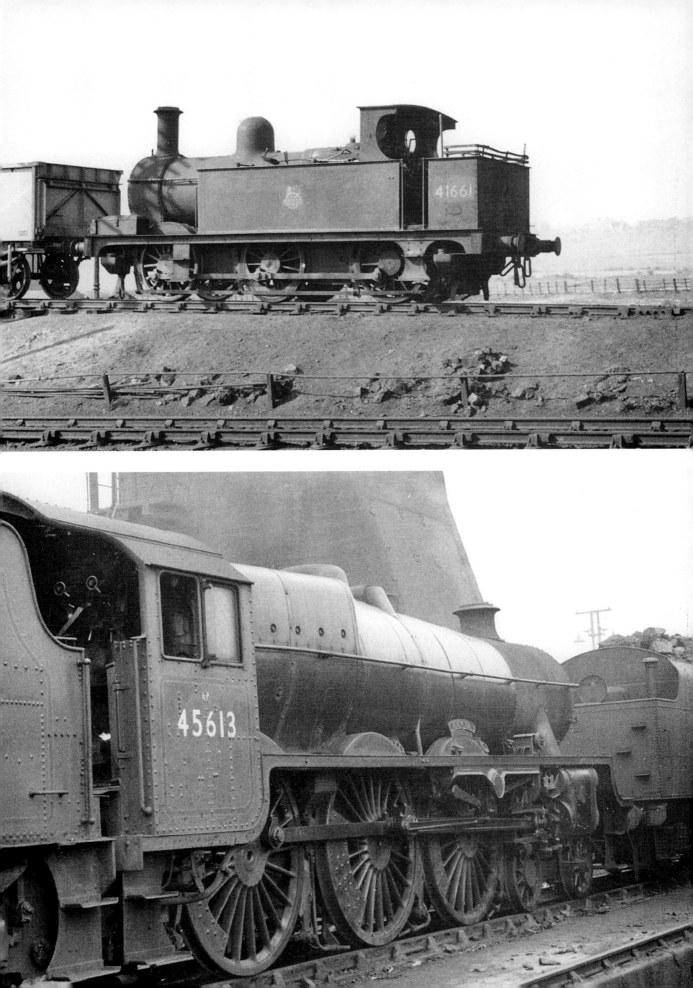

Ex-LNWR 0–8–0 no. 48898 heads north at Leighton Buzzard. The engine was running with a normal tender at this time but it was due for general overhaul and when it returned to Bletchley depot it was complete with a tender cab. No. 48898 had a long history and was rebuilt on several occasions. The sounds produced by these engines when working hard were quite distinctive.

15.7.54

Loose coal lying around made walking in the yard at Huddersfield difficult when this picture of 3F no. 43392 was taken. This depot had a few passenger locomotives in its allocation in the early 1950s, including one 'Jubilee', no. 45596 *Bahamas*, the well-known survivor into preservation.

13.5.56

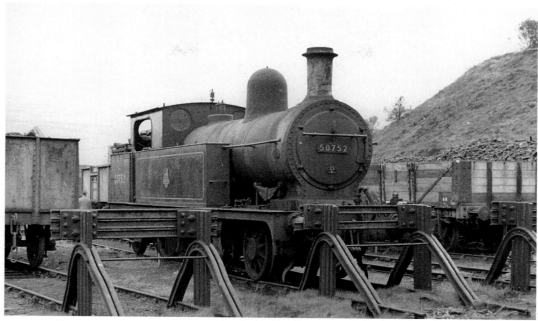

Ex-L&Y 2–4–2T no. 50752 was a Sowerby Bridge locomotive in the mid-1950s. Quite often engines for which there was little work would be dumped at the end of a siding, in some cases never to work again. No. 50752 was an example of those with smaller cylinders. Note also the works plate carried on the side of the smokebox.

13.5.56

Stanier 2–6–4T no. 42659 pictured on shunting duty at Leighton Buzzard. This locomotive was allocated to Bletchley for many years and was often used on the Cambridge line passenger services until these duties were taken over by Standard design tank and tender engines.

15.7.54

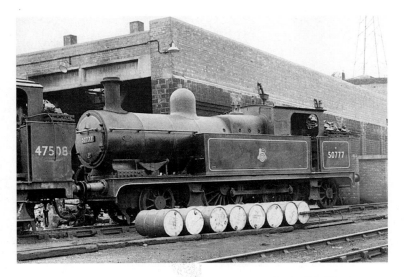

Looking through my 1950s photographs it is amazing how often there appears a row of oil drums. They rarely improve the photograph but it was usually a question of including them or not taking the picture at all. This was the case with ex-L&Y 2–4–2T no. 50777 at Sowerby Bridge depot.

13.5.56

The London Midland Region had a considerable number of WD 2–8–0s. These were mainly to be found in the north of England where they were principally used on colliery traffic. Here nos 90680 and 90621 await their next duty at Huddersfield depot.

13.5.56

Stanier 3MT 2–6–2T no. 40130 pictured at Llandudno. This taper boiler design was a development of the Fowler locomotives introduced five years earlier. Seven of these engines were allocated to Llandudno in the early 1950s and were used principally on local branches and carriage pilot work.

14.8.52

Two 'Crabs' stand at the south end of Rugby station. In the foreground no. 42813 awaits the right away having taken on water, while behind is no. 42840. The distinctive outline of these very useful locomotives, with their small chimneys and large inclined cylinders, can be clearly seen.

5.2.53

The Midland 0–4–4Ts were introduced as early as 1881. No. 58066 was one of those rebuilt with a Belpaire boiler and fitted for push-pull working. By the 1950s only a few remained in active service; this one was photographed at Royston, a depot in the Leeds motive power district.

24.6.56

Even in the mid-1950s locomotives were going into store. Towards the end of the decade numbers increased considerably, and by then most did not even receive the customary tarpaulin round the chimney. This picture of no. 43705, which had not moved for some time, was taken at Royston.

24.6.56

No. 50865, pictured at Huddersfield. The lengthy, rather ungainly outline of the ex-L&Y 2–4–2Ts fitted with longer tanks and large coal capacity can be clearly seen. Time was running out for a number of members of this class when this picture was taken, as many of their duties had already been taken over by more modern engines.

13.5.56

Drifting smoke often made photography difficult. Despite the sunny conditions, the smoke did little to improve this picture of 'Caprotti' class 5 no. 44754 at its home depot, Leeds Holbeck.

13.5.56

The northern end of Bletchley station – a location that will stir the memories of many enthusiasts. Here, rebuilt 'Patriot' class no. 45534 *E. Tootal Broadhurst* thunders through with an express bound for Euston.

20.4.56

(*Opposite top*) Class 2P 4–4–0 no. 40324 was one of a batch built for the Somerset & Dorset Joint Railway and taken into LMS stock in 1930. No. 40324, with its taller pattern chimney, is seen here on carriage pilot duties at Llandudno.

14.8.52

(*Opposite bottom*) The London Midland Region had two classes of 2–6–0 engines classified 5MT. By far the largest were the 'Crabs', introduced in 1926. They were used on numerous duties and during the summer months often worked excursions. No. 42774 was photographed at Manningham depot.

13.5.56

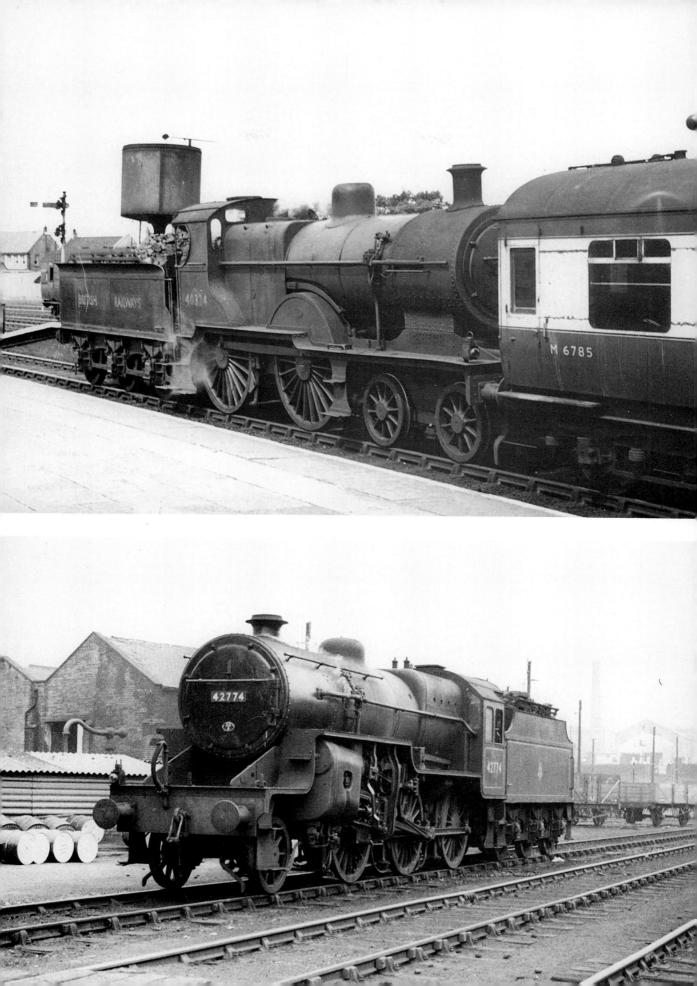

One of the 'Jinties' allocated to Bromsgrove for banking duties was no. 47313, one of seven originally built for the Somerset & Dorset Joint Railway. All were taken into LMS stock in 1930.

17.5.55

Eight 'Jinties' were allocated to Bromsgrove for banking duties. No. 47425 was built in 1927 and withdrawn in 1962. Bromsgrove, shedcode 21C, had an allocation of just twelve engines and in 1958 it was transferred to the Western Region. The 'Jinties' were later replaced by 94xx class 0–6–0PTs.

17.5.55

Early morning at Llandudno and 'Caprotti' class 5 no. 44740 is ready to depart with an express to Crewe. This locomotive was completed in April 1948 and remained in service until March 1963. Several of these Class 5 engines were stored prior to withdrawal.

14.8.52

Already out of service and stored with a 2–6–4T near the spare coal supplies at Bedford shed, 'Compound' no. 41180 still had almost another two years in running stock before it was withdrawn in 1957.

15.5.55

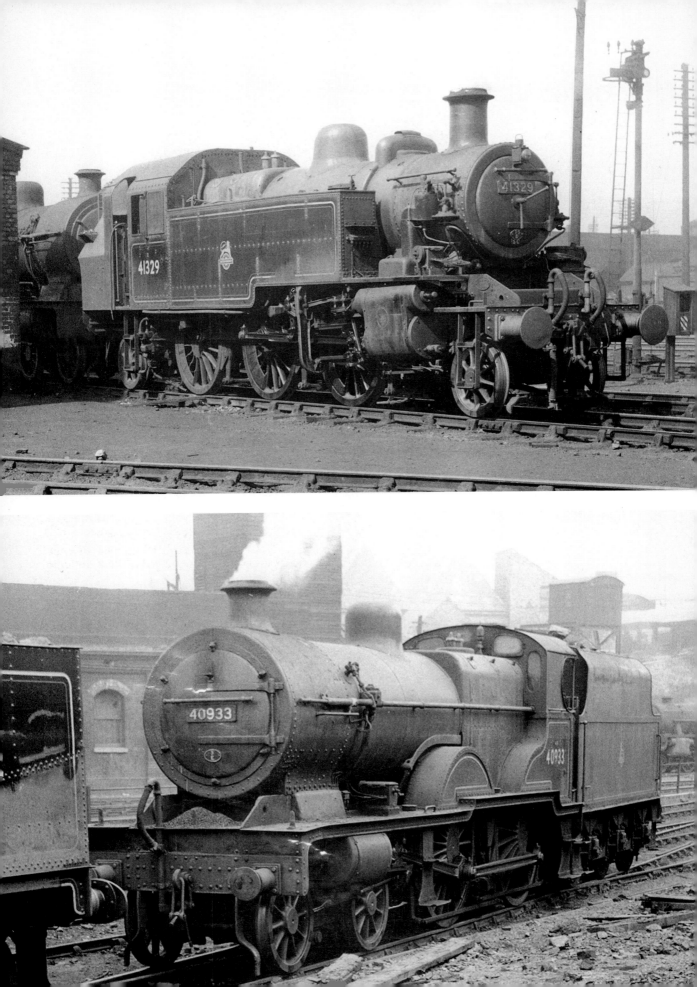

This is Class 2P 4–4–0 no. 40402 shunting horseboxes at Crewe. The engine has received its BR number and the tender is lettered British Railways. The 2Ps built in Midland Railway days were mostly employed on light duties in the early 1950s.

14.8.52

(*Opposite top*) Ivatt 2MT 2–6–2T no. 41329, not completed until May 1952, is seen here at Bedford. It was fitted for push-pull working and was used on Northampton and Hitchin trains. Despite having been in service for just three years when this picture was taken, the chimney had already lost part of the rim. This locomotive had a comparatively short life, being withdrawn in June 1964.

15.5.55

(*Opposite bottom*) 'Compound' no. 40933 is seen here at Monument Lane depot. It is fitted with a curved side tender, which was a standard pattern Fowler 3,500 gallon design; rebuilt as seen here in May 1933, it was not coupled to no. 40933 until 1954. This engine was withdrawn in April 1958.

17.7.55

Fowler 2–6–4T no. 42382 was one of a batch of eleven allocated to Macclesfield depot in the mid-1950s; indeed this class made up this shed's entire allocation of eleven engines. No. 42382 was a long way from its home depot when it was photographed at Monument Lane. It was withdrawn in September 1961.

17.7.55

With over four hundred of the well-known 3F 0–6–0Ts 'Jinties' in service you could not travel far on the London Midland Region before spotting one! This is no. 47509 at Sowerby Bridge depot.

13.5.56

Examples of ex-Midland Railway 3F 0–6–0s were to be found at many depots, most of their duties being pick-up goods and transfer workings. Stourton depot, where this picture of no. 43579 was taken, had a considerable number on its books – the shed's entire allocation consisted of goods and shunting locomotives.

13.5.56

'Caprotti' Class 5 no. 44744 sets out from Bromsgrove on the famous Lickey incline, banked by the famous 0–10–0 no. 58100, widely known as 'Big Bertha'. Built in 1919 by the Midland Railway for this particular duty, no. 58100 completed thirty-seven years' service.

17.7.55

The L&Y 2–4–2T design was introduced in 1889 and a number of examples survived to be taken into British Railways stock. However, by the mid-1950s work for them was becoming scarce, more modern locomotives having taken over many duties. Some 2–4–2Ts found themselves allocated to depots a long way from former L&Y territory. No. 50865 was pictured at Huddersfield, which in pre-Grouping days was a LNWR depot.

13.5.56

(*Opposite top*) Many of the 'Compound' 4P 4–4–0s were withdrawn in the mid-1950s, having been replaced by Standard design locomotives. Time was running out for no. 41079, pictured here at Bedford, as it had just fifteen more months in service.

18.5.55

(*Opposite bottom*) 'Jinties' were constructed at the principal locomotive works of the LMS as well as by private companies. No. 47549, pictured at Bedford MPD, was completed in December 1927 and remained in service until July 1964. These locomotives were the standard shunting design and were to be found at most depots.

15.5.55

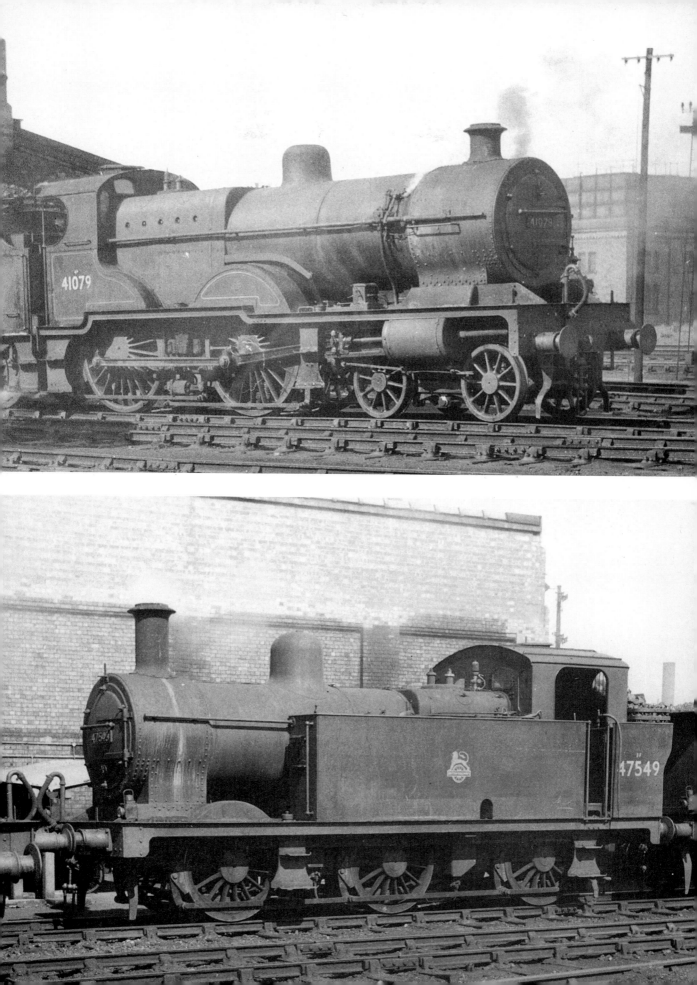

The famous 'Lickey banker', no. 58100, was built at Derby in 1919. This powerful four-cylinder 0–10–0, with a tractive effort of 43,315lb, weighed in at 73 tons and had 4ft 7½in driving wheels. It is seen here on a Sunday morning banking a heavy express headed by Caprotti Class 5 no. 44744. No. 58100 was withdrawn from service in 1956.

17.7.55

(*Opposite top*) Bedford depot had just one 8F in its allocation during the early 1950s. No. 48192, seen here outside the shed, was a Wellingborough engine. It was completed in May 1942 and remained in service until the last year of steam on British Railways, being withdrawn in March.

15.5.55

(*Opposite bottom*) 'Compounds' were still to be found at Bedford in the mid-1950s working London services, but the Standard class 4–6–0s and 4MT 2–6–4Ts introduced around that time soon took over their duties. Here no. 75043 fills up from a typical water crane, with attendant coke brazier alongside. Lighting was provided by a gas lamp.

15.5.55

Unfortunately I did not photograph the old tender standing in front of 3F 0–6–0 no. 43313 at Bedford shed. It was being used as a lime carrier and the LMS lettering was clearly visible. Old tenders were often used in this way – some of them were a great many years old and were once coupled to locomotives long since withdrawn.

15.5.55

(*Opposite top*) Class 5s were not included in Bedford depot's allocation until the mid-1950s, but by the end of the decade it had six. No. 45238 is seen here in the sidings adjacent to the depot. In the background is ex-L&Y 2–4–2T no. 50646, at that time allocated to Wellingborough together with sister engine no. 50650.

15.5.55

(*Opposite bottom*) With the vast slate waste tips in the background, 2MT 2–6–2T no. 41236 stands at Blaenau Ffestiniog ready to work a goods train back to Llandudno. Three 2MTs with consecutive numbers were allocated here during the mid-1950s; all three were still there at the end of the decade and had been joined by five others.

15.8.52

In the mid-1950s Bedford had two Ivatt tanks marking important dates in the history of the class. No. 41272 was the 7,000th locomotive built at Crewe and no. 41329 was the last built. Completion dates were September 1950 and May 1952 respectively. The older engine remained in service for sixteen months longer than no. 41329.

11.9.54

Originally an LMS depot, Plaistow was subsequently transferred to the Eastern Region. During the 1950s the locomotives allocated to this shed (and to the other LTSR depots) were mostly of LMS origin. 'Jinties' nos 47484 and 47311, in typical work-stained condition, await their next duties. This picture and the next are included because of their links with the LMS.

6.5.55

Fresh from works overhaul, almost certainly its last, this is 3P 4–4–2T no. 41945 pictured at Plaistow in the 1950s. This locomotive was one of the batch constructed in LMS days as a development of the original LTSR design. At this time many examples of the class were already in store or little used.

6.5.55

Examples of the 'Jubilee class' were to be seen in many areas of the London Midland Region. No. 45652 *Hawke*, pictured here at Sheffield, was allocated to Trafford Park depot. This engine completed exactly thirty years' service: new in January 1935, it was withdrawn in January 1965.

24.6.56

In their heyday, the 'Compounds' were the principal express engines of the Midland Railway. No. 41049 was completed in LMS days, as were many others. By the mid-1950s these engines were mostly employed on local passenger work. Bedford depot had a considerable number at one time for the London services, until Standards replaced them. No. 41049 stands ready to leave Bedford shed.

11.9.52

(*Opposite top*) Sheffield Grimesthorpe depot closed to steam in 1961. During the mid-1950s it had an allocation of seventy-five locomotives, including several 8F 2–8–0s. One was no. 48189, seen here in a stabling point around a turntable.

24.6.56

(*Opposite bottom*) 'Compound' no. 41062 had obviously run into trouble on its last duty and is seen here at Sheffield with the leading driving wheels removed. Locomotives under repair were frequently to be seen standing in shed yards.

24.6.56

'Jubilee' no. 45674 *Duncan* of Crewe North shed, having just arrived at Llandudno with a special. 'Jubilees', 'Royal Scots', 'Patriots' and Class 5s – the 'Maids of all Work' – were frequent visitors to this popular holiday resort during the summer months.

16.8.52

Class 5MT no. 44732 taking water at Farnley Junction prior to working back to its home shed, Blackpool. It was one of the fireman's duties to climb up on the tender and position the water pipe (often referred to as 'the bag') in the tank while the driver operated the water control.

24.6.56

Twenty of these 0–4–2PTs were built to the design of F.W. Webb for the LNWR between 1896 and 1901. Two survived into BR days, numbered 47862 and 47865. No. 47862 is seen here on shunting duty at Crewe works, where it ended its days.

12.8.52

LNWR 0–8–0 no. 48951 under repair at the back of Bletchley depot. This engine started life as a B class four-cylinder 'Compound' 0–8–0. Completed at Crewe works in August 1904, it was rebuilt as a two-cylinder G1 in October 1923 and in February 1939 was converted to a G2A with 175lb boiler pressure. No. 48951 was one of twelve allocated to the depot.

27.2.55

Class 5 no. 45247 stands at Crewe ready to work a passenger service on the North Wales coast line. Allocated to Holyhead at the time, it was in rather a grubby condition.

12.8.52

(*Opposite top*) Massive inroads were made into the remaining ex-LNWR 'Cauliflowers' shortly after nationalisation. Designed by F.W. Webb, these sturdy locomotives were first introduced in 1887. Many were later rebuilt with Belpaire boilers, as was the case with no. 58377, seen here at Crewe works. In total, 310 of these engines were built between 1880 and 1902.

12.8.52

(*Opposite bottom*) New England WD 2–8–0 no. 90407 and a sister engine, both resplendent in fresh coats of black paint following general overhauls in Crewe works. The WD was an Eastern Region engine allocated to New England. In the background, also ex-works, is 'Jubilee' no. 45633 *Aden* of Preston shed.

12.8.52

Bright early morning sunshine highlights details of 2MT 2–6–2T no. 41237 at Llandudno. This class was introduced by Ivatt for the LMS in 1946, and the last of these engines was constructed in BR days. The design was later used with modifications for the Standard 2–6–2T of the 84xxx series.

14.8.52

(*Opposite top*) Three ex-LNWR 0–8–0s stand in the confined yard at Bletchley shed. The one nearest the camera, no. 48898, is fitted with a tender cab, while another veteran, no. 48952, is next in line. Both of these engines were rebuilt several times during their long working lives.

29.4.56

(*Opposite bottom*) Ready to work a local service to Crewe, Class 5 no. 44836 stands at Llandudno. The young engine-spotter is more interested in the photographer, having doubtless already recorded the number of the Class 5.

14.8.52

When these 0–4–4Ts were introduced by W. Stanier in 1932 they were fitted with a rather ugly stovepipe chimney. Only ten were built, intended to replace older locomotives on push-pull services. As a design, however, these engines never received much attention. No. 41902 was employed on shunting duties at Bletchley in the mid-1950s. Nine of them, including no. 41902, were withdrawn in November 1959. The last survivor, no. 41900, suprisingly remained in service for a further three years.

29.4.56

The 0–6–0s introduced by S.W. Johnson had a long history. The first appeared in 1873 and withdrawals commenced in the 1920s. However, quite a number were still in service at nationalisation, with the last survivors going in the 1960s. These locomotives were used on numerous duties. Kettering depot used them on Cambridge passenger services in the 1950s until sufficient Ivatt 2–6–0s were available to take over all the workings. No. 58188 was photographed at Royston.

24.6.56

Bletchley Class 5s were the usual motive power for the Oxford trains. Here, no. 45004 stands in the down side bay ready to depart. This particular engine was built at Crewe and completed in March 1935. It remained in service until September 1966.

29.4.56

'Patriot' no. 45546 *Fleetwood* was a Willesden engine, one of three allocated to the depot. It is seen here at Crewe North having worked in on a parcels trains. Not all the 'Patriots' were named.

12.8.52

'Royal Scot' class no. 46143 *The South Staffordshire Regiment* awaits its return working at Crewe North depot. The engine is seen here without windshields: the class was fitted with these later. The tender is lettered 'British Railways', as was standard before the emblems were introduced.

12.8.52

(*Opposite top*) The shunter couples up and removes the tail lamp from the coaching stock ready for 2P no. 40324 to leave. This engine was one of a small batch built for the Somerset & Dorset Joint Railway. There were a number of older 2P 4–4–0s still in service during the early 1950s although time was running out for them.

14.8.52

(*Opposite bottom*) By the mid-1950s work was becoming scarce for some of the ex-Midland Railway 4–4–0s and engines were going into store. No. 40411 was stored at Bedford, its chimney protected by a piece of tarpaulin securely tied round it. This locomotive was the only one of its type allocated to Bedford at the time.

11.9.54

In steam days 'Crabs' were frequently called upon to take over from failed locomotives at short notice, whether on passenger or goods trains. These powerful 5MT 2–6–0s with their 5ft 6in driving wheels had a tractive effort greater than the Stanier Class 5s. Nos 42763 and 42756 were photographed at Sheffield Grimesthorpe shed.

24.6.56

Two Class 5s receiving final attention outside Crewe works after a general overhaul; nearest the camera is no. 45406, with no. 44920 in the background. No. 45406 would shortly go to the paint shop. Judging by the pile of new and rotten sleepers in the foreground, some relaying work seems to be under way.

12.8.52

52

Newton Heath Fairburn 2–6–4T no. 42281 and a sister engine await attention in Crewe works. No. 42281 had received its BR number but was still lettered LMS on the tank sides. Visitors to the works were taken round in organised parties, which seldom left sufficient time to explore the yard properly.

12.8.52

Scenes like this were commonplace at many depots in steam days. 'Compound' no. 41105 was undergoing repairs at Rugby with the breakdown crane providing the lift. Note the pile of blocks under the buffer beam: these would certainly have caused a problem if the crane had needed to leave suddenly.

5.2.53

Fresh from general overhaul, 'Jubilee' class no. 45605 *Cyprus* stands in Crewe works yard. These locomotives were classified 6P, with the exception of nos 45735/6, rebuilt with larger boilers and double chimneys, which were classified 7P.

12.8.52

Five of these ex-LNWR 0–6–0STs outlived their classmates for many years, having been transferred to departmental stock. Four went to Wolverton Carriage Works and no. 3323, still retaining its LNWR number, to Crewe. These engines, with their distinctive tall chimneys, were first introduced in 1870; sadly none has survived into preservation.

12.8.52

This ex-LNWR 0–8–0, completed at Crewe in August 1904 as a B class four-cylinder 'Compound', was in the last batch built. In February 1924 it was rebuilt as a G1, and in September 1938 it was converted to a G2A. No. 48952 was photographed at Bletchley, which was home to several members of this class.

29.4.56

The north end of Kettering station was a popular spot for enthusiasts in steam days. From here, movements on the main line could be easily seen, but it also overlooked the locomotive depot located just to the right. Problems could arise when a long goods rumbled through – this 8F no. 48218 temporarily blocked the view of the other lines.

11.4.53

Although it was five years after nationalisation, ex-LNWR 0–8–0 no. 9417 has yet to receive the 4 prefix to its number and to have the LMS lettering removed from its tender. (Not that it mattered as it could barely be seen under a coating of grime anyway.) No. 9417 was photographed shunting at Rugby.

5.2.53

This picture of ex-LNWR 0–8–0 no. 48898 is included principally because it shows clearly the tender cab fitted to this locomotive. The photograph was taken at its home shed, Bletchley. No. 48898 had a long and complicated history. It was built as a class B four-cylinder 'Compound' and was later rebuilt to an F class 2–8–0, then to a G1 0–8–0 and finally, in 1942, to a G2A.

29.4.56

(*Opposite top*) The 4F 0–6–0 design was introduced in 1911 by the Midland Railway, although a great many more were constructed by the LMS. No. 43879, pictured here at Wakefield, was one of the pre-Grouping engines.

13.5.56

(*Opposite bottom*) Five 'Jubilees' were allocated to Farnley Junction depot, including no. 45705 *Seahorse*. This class of 4–6–0s was introduced in 1934 to the design of Sir William Stanier, and four have survived into preservation.

24.6.56

Fowler 4MT no. 42342 of Derby shed departs from a busy Kettering station in a cloud of steam with a northbound local service. On the right, porters are busily loading parcels on to the St Pancras express on the main line platform.

11.4.53

During the 1950s the very common class 3F and 4F 0–6–0s would not have received a second glance from many enthusiasts once they had recorded the number. There were more than a thousand in service and they were to be found at many depots. No. 43181 was photographed at Sheffield Grimethorpe.

24.6.56

Two 3F 0–6–0s await their next turn of duty at Sheffield Grimethorpe. No. 43595 was one of a number of 3Fs allocated to this depot. In addition, there were fifteen of the larger 4F 0–6–0s working from this shed.

24.6.56

During the 1950s fast goods on the London Midland Region were often entrusted to the powerful 5MT 2–6–0 'Crabs', which were capable of a fair turn of speed. Here, no. 42798 passes Kettering on the main line on its journey to London.

11.4.53

Fifteen 'Patriot' class 4–6–0s were to be found working from Crewe North depot; no. 45543 *Home Guard* was one of them. All but two members of this class were of new construction although they were officially regarded as rebuilds. The first two locomotives were rebuilds of LNWR 'Claughtons'. Some 'Patriots' were later rebuilt by H. Ivatt.

12.8.52

(*Opposite top*) Class 5 no. 44971, pictured at Crewe North depot, fitted with a self-weighing tender. Tests were frequently carried out during the 1950s with various locomotives recording coal and water consumption on different duties and routes.

12.8.52

(*Opposite bottom*) Many locomotives were still to be seen running with their tenders lettered LMS in 1952. Accrington depot 'Crab' no. 42796 was one of them. It was photographed at Crewe North ready for a return working.

12.8.52

Something must have gone wrong during running-in trials on Caprotti Class 5 no. 44755 as it had only just received a general overhaul. It is seen here under repair at Crewe North with the front bogie removed. This engine was one of three fitted with double chimneys.

12.8.52

(*Opposite top*) Class 5 no. 45001 was one of the batch built at Crewe works and completed in 1935. It was allocated to Mold Junction and was photographed heading an express at Llandudno. It was one of the Class 5s withdrawn in 1968, just five months before the end of steam on BR.

10.8.52

(*Opposite bottom*) Scenes like this were commonplace in steam days, with locomotives under repair in the yards. Here, 'Patriot' no. 45507 *Royal Tank Corps* is pictured at Crewe North awaiting the return of its bogie. Quite often repairs were carried out completely in the open if covered space was at a premium. Note the condition of the shed roof.

12.8.52

Caprotti class 5 no. 44748 was just four years old when this picture was taken at Crewe North shed. The locomotive was in a terrible external condition. No. 44748 remained in service until July 1964.

12.8.52

'Compound' no. 41114 is seen here at Rhyl on its way to Llandudno. Note the special reporting number on the smokebox. No. 41114 was completed in December 1925 and withdrawn in May 1958.

10.8.52

Devons Road shed (1D) had six of these Ivatt 2–6–0s in its allocation, including the first two built and completed in 1947. No. 43020, seen here, was ready for service in December 1948, several months after nationalisation. The last member of the class was completed in September 1952.

6.5.55

Class 4F no. 44348, photographed at Devons Road shed, was fitted with automatic train control. This locomotive was built by Kerr Stuart and completed in April 1927. It remained in service until July 1964.

6.5.55

The 3F 0–6–2T design was introduced in 1903 by R.H. Whitelegg. Fourteen were built for the LT&SR but they received little attention even after this railway was absorbed by the Midland. Ten were originally named, but the names were removed shortly after the LT&SR was taken over. The class had a long life, becoming extinct in 1962.

6.5.55

(*Opposite top*) Amid clouds of escaping steam, 2P 4–4–0 no. 40536 leaves Kettering with a northbound local passenger service. These engines, with their 7ft 0in driving wheels could certainly get a move on when the occasion arose.

31.5.52

(*Opposite bottom*) This was the end of the road for ex-LNWR 'Cauliflower' no. 58426. Pictured at Crewe North depot, it was awaiting transfer to the works for scrapping. Years of hard work were clearly evident and the shedcode plate had already been removed.

12.8.52

The 'Compounds', with their 6ft 9in driving wheels, were first class express engines in their heyday. In British Railways days they were principally used on semi-fasts and cross-country routes. No. 40930, in good external condition, is seen here leaving Bournville.

17.7.55

(*Opposite top*) Wakefield depot, shedcode 25A, was the principal shed of the district with just over one hundred locomotives on its books in the mid-1950s. As it was a former Lancashire & Yorkshire Railway depot it was not surprising to find ex-L&Y 3F 0–6–0s present. No. 52411 is seen here next to a WD 2–8–0 – there were no fewer than sixty-seven WD 2–8–0s to be found at Wakefield.

13.5.56

(*Opposite bottom*) During the early 1950s many of the St Pancras local services were worked by Bedford 'Compounds'. All this changed when Standard class 4MT 2–6–4Ts and class 4MT 4–6–0s were allocated to the depot and soon took over many services. No. 41049 was photographed in the shed yard.

15.5.55

The Stanier 3MT 2–6–2 tank no. 40165 was allocated to Bedford shed for many years, and was the sole example of its class to be found there. On the numerous occasions I visited the shed it was usually standing in the yard.

15.5.55

(*Opposite top*) Bedford depot had a considerable number of 3F 0–6–0s on its books. Their duties included shunting and local trip working at the nearby brickyards. These engines were originally introduced by the Midland Railway in 1885 and from 1920 onwards were rebuilt with Belpaire boilers. No. 43529 is pictured at Bedford.

15.5.55

(*Opposite bottom*) The fireman takes advantage of a stop at Kettering to break and bring forward coal before setting out again on the journey north. No. 40543 was an example of the Midland Railway design built between 1882 and 1901 and rebuilt with superheaters from 1912 onwards.

31.5.52

Crewe works had its own locomotive allocation for shunting duties. Two of these engines are pictured here in the works yard: ex-Caledonian 'Pug' 0–4–0ST no. 56032 and ex-LNWR 'Cauliflower' no. 58377. The latter class was built at Crewe, and several examples ended their days on shunting duties.

12.8.52

Class 8F no. 48107 heads north through Kettering on the main line with a heavy iron ore train. At this time a number of iron stone quarries were operational in this part of Northamptonshire, all long since closed.

31.5.52

Willesden had a number of ex-LNWR 0–8–0s on its books, including the work-stained no. 49277 pictured here awaiting coaling. This was built as a G1 in 1917 and rebuilt to a G2A in August 1947. These very useful and powerful locomotives had a long history.

9.9.51

Ivatt class 2MT no. 41272 was the 7,000th locomotive built at Crewe works, and was completed in 1950. Small plates commemorating this were carried on the tank side below the emblems. The engine is seen here at its home depot, Bedford, but it spent its final years in the West Country before withdrawal in October 1965.

11.9.54

Trials were conducted on a regular basis during the 1950s, with various locomotives using a self-weighing tender. This provided information on coal consumption with various loads and types of duty over different routes. Class 5 no. 44986 was photographed at a smoky Holbeck with one of these tenders fitted.

13.5.56

You never quite knew what locomotives you would find at Bletchley shed. There could be express passenger engines under repair and locomotives passing through on transfer or on their way to works for overhaul. WD 2–8–0 no. 90136 was a complete stranger as it was an Eastern Region engine allocated to Colwick. Immediately behind it in the gloom stands a North London outside cylinder 0–6–0T – how I wish their positions were reversed!

29.4.56

Bedford had just one ex-Midland Railway 2F 0–6–0, no. 58305, in its allocation for many years. It is seen here at its home depot and appears to have had a general overhaul recently. This particular locomotive retained the more open Johnson cab.

11.9.54

8F 2–8–0 no. 48304 pounds through Kettering station with a northbound goods while a 2MT 2–6–0 stands in the main line platform. Before the introduction of the Standard 9F 2–10–0s, 8Fs and Beyer-Garratt 2–6–6–2Ts worked the heavy mineral trains.

31.5.52

The ex-LNWR 'Cauliflowers' had long since gone from the Keswick line when this Ivatt 2–6–0 no. 46455 was photographed on its way back to Penrith with a pick-up goods, by that stage consisting of just a brake van.

9.63

Sunshine and shade at Bedford shed, with 3F 0–6–0 no. 43785. This locomotive was one of the batch introduced by R.M. Deeley for the Midland Railway in 1906. It was subsequently rebuilt with a Belpaire boiler.

11.9.54

While not one of my best pictures technically, this photograph has been included to show the variety of engines to be found at Rhyl depot in 1952. WD 2–8–0 no. 90212 was an example of those which had been 'westernised'.

10.8.52

The Standard class 5s were introduced in 1951, and when this picture of no. 73024 was taken at Rhyl they were still relatively new. The tractive effort of the standard design was 26,120lb as compared to 25,455lb of the Stanier design, while the driving wheels were 6ft and 6ft 2in respectively.

10.8.52

(*Opposite top*) In 1928 the LMS introduced a development of the Midland 2P 4–4–0 design, with reduced mountings and various modified dimensions. The new locomotives were used on many duties including local passenger, cross-country services and, on occasions, as pilots on expresses. This is no. 40679, photographed at Rhyl depot.

10.8.52

(*Opposite bottom*) The London Midland Region extended as far as Godmanchester. Here, Ivatt 2MT no. 46404 is seen leaving Huntingdon East with the Kettering to Cambridge service. These locomotives replaced ageing Johnson 0–6–0s on this service and soon became popular with the Kettering enginemen.

8.2.53

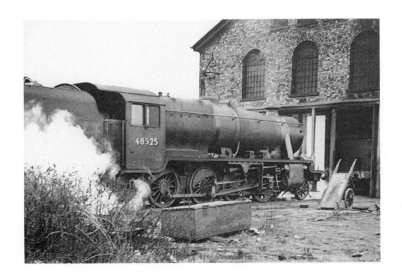

Rugby depot had a small locomotive repair works adjacent to the shed building. Here, 8F no. 48525 stands outside under test following attention in the works. Note the untidy site.

5.2.53

The first five lightweight Ivatt 2MT 2–6–0s were allocated to Kettering to replace ageing Johnson 0–6–0s on the Cambridge services. During the following years three more Ivatts and two Standard 78xxx series engines joined them. No. 46400 is seen here in front of the Kettering coaling plant.

31.5.52

Frequently locomotives could be found undergoing repairs in shed yards, as was the case with Camden's 'Princess Coronation' no. 46242 *City of Glasgow*, pictured at Willesden with its front bogie removed. The weight of the front end is supported by wooden blocks.

9.9.51

Many of the St Pancras local services in the early 1950s were worked by Bedford depot 'Compounds'. No. 41198 had just arrived at Bedford Midland with a train from London. This engine was the penultimate member of the class, completed in March 1927. It was a fairly early withdrawal, being condemned in December 1955.

23.2.52

Two LNWR 0–8–0s await their next turn of duty at Willesden. No. 48953 was a visitor with a long history. Built in 1896 as an A class three-cylinder 'Compound' 0–8–0, it was rebuilt to a C class simple in November 1904. In 1926 it was rebuilt again, this time to a G1, and then converted to a G2A in December 1939.

9.9.51

Fresh from works overhaul, WD 2–8–0 no. 90194 was photographed at Willesden resplendent in a shiny coat of black paint – which doubtless would soon be hidden by grime. There were no WDs in Willesden's allocation so this must be a visitor.

9.9.51

Several members of the 'Patriot' class never carried names. No. 45547, seen here at a smoky Camden depot, was one of these. In the background is 'Princess Coronation' no. 46225 *Duchess of Gloucester*.

9.9.51

Rhyl depot was of LNWR origin. During the 1950s examples of the 0–6–0 'Cauliflowers' and 0–6–2T designs were still to be found there. No. 28589 was still carrying its LMS number at the time this picture was taken. It had just four months service left before it made its final journey to Crewe works.

10.8.52

Two of these ex-LNWR 0–6–0 'Cauliflowers' were still at Rhyl in 1952. No. 58362 had received its BR number, but the other example still carried its old LMS number. These engines were first introduced in 1887.

10.8.52

Of the many depots I visited during the 1950s Rhyl always stands out for the variety of locomotives to be found there. Here, ex-L&Y no. 52453 stands in the yard accompanied by two ex-LNWR 'Cauliflowers'. Also on shed were LNWR 2–4–2Ts, several engines of Midland and LMS origin, Standards and even a WD 2–8–0.

10.8.52

(*Opposite top*) Several ex-L&Y 0–6–0s were to be found at depots on the North Wales coast line in the early 1950s. No. 52356 was one of those allocated to Rhyl. This class first made its appearance in 1889, designed by J.A.F. Aspinall.

10.8.52

(*Opposite bottom*) In 1890 the first of the 1P 2–4–2Ts designed by F.W. Webb emerged from Crewe works. In all, 160 were built over a seven-year period. Withdrawals commenced in 1921, with three going before the Grouping. Forty-three survived to be taken into British Railways stock. After this numbers decreased rapidly, with the last survivor being withdrawn in 1955. No. 46643, with its tank still lettered LMS, was photographed at Rhyl.

10.8.52

The 175 Fowler 7F 0–8–0s were introduced in 1929 as a development of the very useful G2 LNWR 0–8–0s. Unfortunately they were nowhere near as successful. Withdrawals commenced in 1949, with the last survivors going in 1960. No. 49538 had already been condemned and was awaiting scrapping at Harwich works.

22.9.57

Patricroft depot, shedcode 10C, was of LNWR origin and was a sizable shed with an allocation of around seventy-four engines. These included several 'Jubilees' and a large number of Class 5s. There were also several ex-L&Y 0–6–0s but no. 52389 was a visitor from Bolton.

22.9.57

Stanier 8F 2–8–0 no. 48612 was one of a batch built at Ashford works. Completed in July 1943, it remained in service until the last year of steam on BR, being withdrawn in June. It is seen here pounding up Shap, assisted by a Fairburn 2–6–4T banker.

9.63

The first two 'Patriots' were rebuilds of the LNWR 'Claughton' class, and they retained their original wheels and some other parts. No. 45500 *Patriot*, pictured here at Patricroft shed, was a visitor from Carlisle Kingmoor depot. It was rebuilt with no. 45501 in 1930 and remained in service until March 1961.

22.9.57

The distinctive 1ft 6in gauge 0–4–0ST *Wren* was built by Beyer Peacock in 1887 for the L&YR and was used on the extensive narrow gauge system at Horwich works. It was still in use in 1957, when this picture was taken, and fortunately this very interesting locomotive has been preserved as part of the National Collection at York.

22.9.57

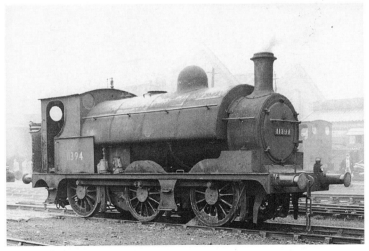

Shunting work at Horwich works was in the hands of a number of ex-L&Y 0–6–0STs in departmental stock. No. 11394 still carried its LMS number but had received a BR emblem on the tank side. These engines were rebuilds of 0–6–0 tender locomotives.

22.9.57

'Jubilee' class no. 45614 *Leeward Islands*, a Kentish Town engine, is pictured here at Trafford Park ready for its return working to London. Built in 1934, it completed almost thirty years' service before withdrawal.

22.9.57

Willesden was a large depot with over 140 locomotives on its books in the early 1950s, mostly freight engines. 3F 0–6–0 no. 43453 was a stranger – and it was a long way from home, being allocated to Toton depot.

9.9.51

When the lightweight Ivatt 2–6–0s were introduced they took over many duties previously performed by much older engines. The 2MTs showed considerable improvements, not least of which was the more comfortable cab, and were much liked by enginemen, especially those who were used to engines with open draughty cabs. No. 46430 was photographed at Rhyl.

10.8.52

(*Opposite top*) Patricroft shed had well over thirty Stanier Class 5s and two Standard Class 5s in the mid-1950s. No. 73094 was one of them, pictured here at its home depot.

22.9.57

(*Opposite bottom*) The large-diameter driving wheels fitted to the Midland 2P 4–4–0s can be clearly seen in this picture of no. 40463 at Bristol Barrow Road depot. Unfortunately no examples of 2P design built by the Midland Railway (or the later LMS post-Grouping development) have survived into preservation.

31.8.55

Ex-L&Y 0–6–0 no. 52431 was one of those rebuilt from 1911 onwards with Belpaire boiler and extended smokebox, which gave the rebuilds a very different appearance from the rest of the class. No. 52431 was photographed at Bolton shed.

16.10.55

(*Opposite top*) Ten of these Franco-Crosti 9F 2–10–0s were built. Nos 92020–92029 were all allocated to Wellingborough, where this picture of no. 92026 was taken. It shows the main boiler barrel with the pre-heater drum below. These engines failed to meet expectations and were later rebuilt.

22.7.56

(*Opposite bottom*) Franco-Crosti no. 92026 at Wellingborough. The exhaust on these engines was situated halfway along the boiler, while the chimney in the conventional position was used only for raising steam, after which it was blanked off. These engines soon became unpopular because of the unpleasant working conditions caused by smoke and fumes drifting on to the footplate.

22.7.56

Several ex-L&Y 0–6–0STs were to be found at Bolton. In all, 230 were originally built as 0–6–0 tender locomotives and rebuilt to saddle tanks during the period 1891–1900. Withdrawals commenced in 1926, but 101 survived into BR service, with the last being withdrawn in 1964.

16.10.55

(*Opposite top*) Bristol Barrow Road, shedcode 22A, was a sizable depot of Midland Railway origin with around fifty-five engines in the mid-1950s. Standard Class 5 no. 73028, in a very work-stained condition, is pictured in the yard.

31.8.55

(*Opposite bottom*) These 3MT parallel boiler 2–6–2Ts were introduced by H. Fowler in 1930 and were widely distributed over the system. No. 40009 is seen here at Trafford Park. Nineteen were fitted with condensing gear for working on Moorgate services.

22.9.57

Fowler 7F 0–8–0 no. 49538 pictured in the depths of Bolton shed. I was to photograph this same engine two years later, when it was awaiting the cutter's torch.

16.10.55

(*Opposite top*) Fairburn 2–6–4T no. 42064 stands ready for its next working at its home depot, Trafford Park. The Fairburn engines were a development of the Stanier design, with a shorter wheelbase and other detail alterations.

22.9.57

(*Opposite bottom*) Two express passenger locomotives of different eras stand ready for the next duty at Trafford Park. 'Compound' no. 41116 was one of the depot's allocation, while Class 5 no. 45260 was a visitor from Carlisle. Note the row of oil cans on the Compound's footplate.

16.10.55

Ex-L&Y 0–6–0 engines were to be found at many depots. No. 52095, seen here at Rose Grove shed, was in a work-stained condition, typical of the 1950s. These engines were a highly successful class.

22.9.57

(*Opposite top*) Stanier two-cylinder 2–6–4T no. 42469 pictured on shed duties at Trafford Park. Note the piles of ash on the front of the running plate. The locomotive remained in service until May 1963.

16.10.55

(*Opposite bottom*) 'Compounds' in their heyday were to be seen at the head of many principal express trains on the Midland Railway. By the 1950s they had been relegated to secondary duties. No. 41170, seen here at Trafford Park, appears to have done little work in recent months.

16.10.55

In 1964 Kettering shed was a shadow of its former self, with Class 5s, 8Fs and 9F 2–10–0s being the only locomotives likely to be seen still in service. Numerous other engines were to be seen at times in the shed yard, withdrawn and on their way to Cohens scrapyard nearby. No. 44828 still had another three years in service when this picture was taken.

18.10.64

100

(*Above*) No. 49433 is a typical example of the ex-LNWR 0–8–0s in the 1950s. These were very long-lived and powerful engines which were well known for the whistling and wheezing sounds they produced when in action.

22.7.56

(*Below*) Ex-LNWR G2 class 0–8–0 no. 49433 was completed in November 1921. The cab and rivet detail on the tender can be clearly seen in this picture, taken at Rugby depot.

22.7.56

On Sundays in the 1950s a long row of goods engines, mostly 8F 2–8–0s and ex-LNWR 0–8–0s, could be seen at Northampton depot. No. 49366 started life as a B class four-cylinder 'Compound' in October 1903; it was converted to a G1 in October 1921 and to a G2A in December 1935.

5.9.54

(*Opposite top*) The ex-LNWR 0–8–0s had a long and complex history in many cases. No. 49078, seen here at Toton depot, started life as a two-cylinder G class; it was converted to a G1 in December 1932 and seven years later to a G2A. These engines did not carry smokebox number plates.

4.4.54

(*Opposite bottom*) Class 5 no. 44828 was a Leeds Holbeck engine. It was one of the Crewe-built engines constructed towards the end of the Second World War. Completed in July 1944, it remained in service until September 1967.

16.10.55

Carlisle depot Class 5 no. 45323 going well on the long climb up Shap with a fast goods. Only on rare occasions, when an engine was in trouble, would a banker be called upon for passenger and fast goods. This Class 5 remained in service until September 1967, completing over thirty years' service.

9.63

The Shap bankers were mostly 2–6–4Ts when this picture of Fairburn no. 42110 was taken at Tebay shed. Standing on the adjacent line is a Fowler 2–6–4T, also on banking duties. Only one line ran in each direction over Shap, so in busy periods freights could be held at Tebay for some time.

9.63

Standard class 2MT 2–6–2T no. 84020 in store at Llandudno Junction shed. The chimney is protected by a piece of tarpaulin. A fresh coat of black paint has been applied to the smokebox and chimney.

11.7.64

Two Shap bankers at Tebay shed await the call to assist a heavy northbound goods train on the long exposed climb to the summit. On the left is Fowler 2–6–4T no. 42414, with Fairburn 2–6–4T no. 42110 alongside.

9.63

'Royal Scot' no. 46101 *Royal Scots Grey* of Camden depot is seen here making heavy weather of its journey across Anglesey with a London-bound express. Withdrawals of this class commenced in 1962, with no. 46101 lasting until August 1963.

18.7.60

Most of the locomotives allocated to Tebay shed were used for banking duties on Shap. Fowler 2–6–4T no. 42414 was one of a batch built at Derby with side-window cabs; completed in November 1933, it was in service for almost thirty-one years.

9.63

Class 5 no. 44769 had worked a special from Liverpool to Llandudno, and when this picture was taken it had been serviced ready for its return working to its home depot, Edge Hill. During the summer Llandudno shed serviced numerous visitors working in on specials and excursions.

11.7.64

A seven-coach local service headed by Fairburn 2–6–4T tank no. 42240, photographed near Penmaenmawr on its way to Bangor. The North Wales coast line presented no problems to a locomotive in good condition.

16.7.64

(*Opposite top*) There were few sheds that did not have at least one 'Jinty' in their allocation. No. 47598 was photographed at Llandudno Junction during the early 1950s. This shed for many years had just one, but by the end of the decade, and almost up to closure, the number had increased to three.

11.7.64

(*Opposite bottom*) Work was scarce for several engines at Llandudno Junction by 1964 and a number were placed in store. 4F no. 44525 and Standard 2MT no. 84020 were left in an isolated siding, but how long they remained there is not known. The 4F was withdrawn in October 1966.

11.7.64

Caprotti Standard Class 5 no. 73144 photographed at Llandudno shed. This depot was of LNWR origin and closed in 1966. The Standard Class 5s were a good design but they always seemed to be overshadowed by the 'Black Fives'.
11.7.64

(*Opposite top*) The pick-up freight was once a familiar sight throughout the country, calling at numerous stations where the locomotive performed any shunting as required. Here Ivatt 2–6–2T no. 41234 trundles across Anglesey on its way back to Bangor.

18.7.60

(*Opposite bottom*) Class 5 no. 45333 seen here at its home depot, Wellingborough. This was one of 327 built by Armstrong Whitworth; completed in March 1937, it remained in service until June 1966. Locomotives of this class were also built by the Vulcan Foundry and at the LMS locomotive works.

18.10.64

Several of these 4F 0–6–0s were to be found at Workington depot, a small shed with just twenty-eight locomotives in the mid-1950s, including nos 44035 and 44305. I wonder how often mistakes were made when writing down these numbers!

9.63

The 'Midland line' from Peterborough to Leicester runs alongside the east coast main line for the first few miles. Standard class 4 4–6–0 no. 75040 of Leicester depot heads a typical four-coach train near Walton, Peterborough. Some of the services had already been taken over by diesel multiple units by this time.

6.9.62

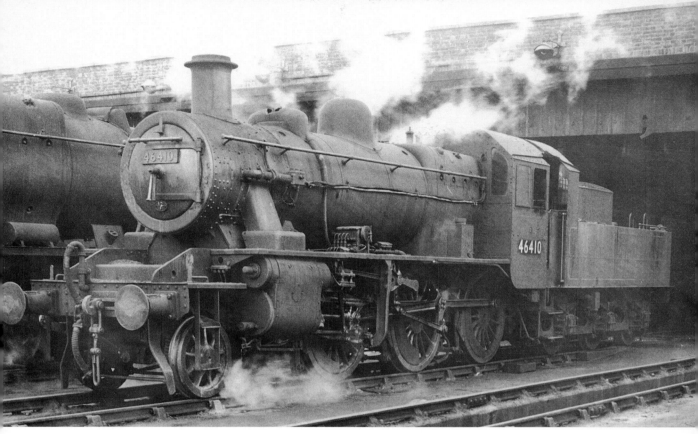

The first ten examples of the very useful lightweight Ivatt 2–6–0s emerged from Crewe works in December 1946. No. 46410, seen here at Workington, was the first of the second batch of ten built in LMS days at Crewe.

9.63

Class 5 no. 44708 had worked into Llandudno with a holiday special. The engine was photographed at Llandudno Junction shed, where it was turned, coaled and watered ready for its return journey. Note the two reporting numbers on the smokebox. Visitors from a considerable distance were serviced at this shed during the summer months.

11.7.64

Fowler 2–6–4T no. 42405 was fitted with a side-window cab. This picture was taken at Mirfield during a RCTS visit. Those interested purely in numbers can be seen going into the shed; such was the timing of these visits that photographs had to be taken quickly. It was amazing just how quickly some members of the party could be ready for the next shed.

13.5.56

(*Opposite top*) The run down Shap to Tebay gave the fireman a chance to relax on Class 5 no. 45284 heading a train of steel coils. Steam was still fairly common on goods and occasional passenger trains at this time but the principal expresses were firmly in the hands of diesel power.

9.63

(*Opposite bottom*) Weak winter sunshine highlights Standard class 2MT no. 84006 at Wellingborough. This engine and two others were mostly employed on push-pull branch line workings. The Standard 2MTs were based on the Ivatt design with BR modifications.

15.11.64

'Britannia' class no. 70024 *Vulcan* (with nameplates removed) has just turned at Crewe South shed. The notice warns 'locomotives must not run onto this turntable at speed greater than two miles per hour'.

16.10.66

(*Opposite top*) This picture of Ivatt 2–6–0 no. 43135 at Stourton shed shows clearly the high running plate on these engines. This design (with some modifications) was used for the Standard class 4MT 2–6–0s. No. 43135 was built at Horwich Works and completed in December 1951. It was in service for just fifteen years.

20.3.66

(*Opposite bottom*) The Standard class 2MT 2–6–0s were based on the Ivatt design of 1946 with some BR modifications. These very useful lightweight locomotives had a tractive effort of 18,515lb and were designed for branch and cross-country services. No. 78031 was photographed at Crewe South.

16.10.66

Rebuilt 'Patriot' no. 45526 *Morecambe and Heysham* seen here at Carlisle Upperby shed one month before it was withdrawn. Built in 1933, it was rebuilt with a double chimney and type 2A taper boiler in February 1947. Rebuilding reclassified these engines as 7P with a tractive effort of 29,570lb.
18.9.64

Only one example of the very useful Ivatt 4MT 2–6–0 design has been preserved. No. 43077 is pictured here at Royston depot. This locomotive was one of the batch built at Darlington works and was completed in October 1950, well into BR days. It remained in service until April 1967.

20.3.66

These short-wheelbase 0–4–0Ts were introduced by the Midland Railway to the design of R.M. Deeley in 1907. They were used for shunting work where restricted access and tight curves existed. No. 41533 was among the withdrawn engines at Canklow shed when this picture was taken on a rather gloomy day.

8.4.66

Locomotives withdrawn from running stock were often used for shunting duties at Crewe works. No. 47658 carries the W1 duty plate above its buffer beam. Although the smokebox number plate is still fitted, the number on the side had been painted out.

16.10.66

(*Opposite top*) Most of the principal Scottish express trains had already been taken over by diesels in 1963, although steam was still to be seen on some trains. Here, Class 5 no. 44937 tackles Shap unaided with a nine-coach express.

9.63

(*Opposite bottom*) Among the last Class 5s to receive a general overhaul was no. 44819, seen here at Crewe works. Although the Derby-built engine received attention at this late stage it only remained in service until December 1967.

16.10.66

Ivatt 2MT no. 46443, pictured here at Crewe South depot, is one of the lucky survivors. It was completed at Crewe in February 1950 and remained in service until March 1967.

16.10.66

Two withdrawn 1F 0–6–0Ts at Canklow depot with no. 41765 nearest the camera and no. 41804 at the back. No. 41765 was one of those with the open cab widely known as 'half cabs'.

8.4.66

These short wheelbase 0–4–0STs were a Kitson design modified to LMS requirements. Five were built by Kitsons in 1932. Although the BR number 47001 is visible on the cabside the earlier and larger LMS number 7001 is more prominent.

8.4.66

Most of the Class 5s still in service in 1966 were in appalling external condition. No. 45219 was photographed at Royston. This locomotive was completed in November 1935 by Armstrong Whitworth and withdrawn in September 1967.

20.3.66

Fairburn 2–6–4T no. 42110 pounds up Shap banking a heavy north-bound goods headed by an 8F. Once over the summit the banker would fall back, cross over and run back light engine to Tebay ready for its next trip.

9.63

(*Opposite top*) Fairburn 2–6–4T no. 42138 was still in reasonable external condition when this picture was taken at Manningham. This engine was completed at Derby in March 1950 and managed just over seventeen years' service.

20.3.66

(*Opposite bottom*) 'Jubilee' class no. 45627 *Sierra Leone* of Derby shed crossing Anglesey in fine style with an express from Holyhead. Withdrawals of the 'Jubilees' commenced in 1961; no. 45627 soldiered on until September 1966.

18.7.60

Class 8F no. 48045 of Mansfield depot in typical grubby state of most heavy goods locomotives in the mid-1960s. Note the pile of ash on the front of the running plate – it was presumably still there when the engine left the shed.

11.10.64

With steam leaking from several places, 'Britannia' class no. 70024 *Vulcan*, minus nameplates, leaves Crewe South shed. Completed in October 1951, this engine spent much of its life on the Western Region, ending up at Carlisle Kingmoor depot. It was withdrawn in December 1967 and cut up by T.W. Ward at Killamarsh.

16.10.66

In 1966 a very interesting collection of withdrawn locomotives could be seen at Canklow depot. They included several ex-Midland Railway 1F 0–6–0Ts, a design dating back to 1878. No. 41804 was one of those known as 'half cabs'.

8.4.66

Skipton shed was transferred to the North Eastern Region in the 1960s, and 4F no. 44570 was one of the many ex-LMS designs still to be found there in the final days of steam. Time was running out for this engine as it was withdrawn in October 1965.

9.63

Another withdrawn 1F 0–6–0T at Canklow was no. 41734. This engine had the more conventional cab which offered better protection for the enginemen. The front numberplate had already been removed.

8.4.66

'Britannia' class no. 70016 *Ariel* had already lost its nameplates when this picture was taken at Leeds Holbeck. Much of the engine's working life had been on the Western Region. Its last shed was Carlisle Kingmoor from where it was withdrawn in August 1967 and subsequently cut up by J. McWilliams, Shettleston.

20.3.66

The fireman on Class 5 no. 45257 heading a Holyhead express had time to admire the view as it neared Penmaenmawr. Locomotives never needed to work hard on this gently graded route.

14.7.64

Standard class 9F 2–10–0 no. 92006 pictured at Normanton depot. The original locomotives of this class were fitted with single chimneys, but some were later to receive a double blastpipe and chimney as seen here.

20.3.66

By the mid-1960s it was becoming rare to see a clean steam locomotive unless it was one of the few still receiving works attention. Class 5 no. 44854 at Stourton, with eighteen months' service left, was in typical condition for the period.

20.3.66

The rebuilt 'Crosti' engines still had an unconventional appearance, although gone were the problems caused by smoke, fumes and steam entering the footplate which created dangerous and unpleasant conditions. No. 92020 is pictured at Kettering.

13.12.64

(*Opposite*) Several withdrawn express passenger locomotives were present at Carlisle Upperby shed in 1964. 'Royal Scot' no. 46110 *Grenadier Guardsman* had been withdrawn in February that year. The coupling rods had been removed and the motion dismantled ready for its last journey, although surprisingly the nameplate and front numberplate were still on the engine.

18.9.64

Standard Class 5 no. 73069 was used on several enthusiasts' specials in the last months of steam on British Railways. It had recently worked a 'special', judging by the white painted buffers, most of which had rubbed off. The rest of the engine was not particularly clean when this picture was taken at Bolton.

17.3.68

(*Opposite top*) Many of the remaining steam engines still working in the final years of steam were in a deplorable state – but this was not the case with Standard Class 5 no. 73040 photographed at Bolton. It was in good external condition, and presumably had been cleaned to work a 'special'.

17.3.68

(*Opposite bottom*) The running plate near the buffer beam was showing signs of damage on no. 42782, pictured at Birkenhead. The majority of the locomotives present at this depot during my visit were Standard designs.

16.10.66

Only three examples of the 245-strong 5MT class known as 'Crabs' have survived into preservation. No. 42765, seen here at Birkenhead, was one of them. Standing behind was another member of the class, no. 42782, which was not so lucky.

16.10.66

242

The rebuilt 'Crosti' 9F 2–10–0s were less powerful than conventional members of the class and were classified 8F. No. 92023 was photographed at Birkenhead with just one year left in service.

16.10.66

During a short stay at Keswick I twice had the opportunity of photographing the return morning pick-up goods on its way back with just a brake van. Unfortunately, the engine was no. 46455 on both occasions.

9.63

Withdrawn locomotives were to be seen at numerous depots during the 1960s, eventually being towed away four or five at a time to a scrapyard. Carnforth depot had a number of condemned engines, including Standard Class 4MT no. 75034 with a rather battered cylinder cover.

17.3.68

(*Opposite top*) Standard 9F 2–10–0 no. 92223 was among the last members of the class in service. It is seen here at Carnforth shed on a blustery early spring day just a few months before steam finished on British Railways.

17.3.68

(*Opposite bottom*) Derby-built Class 5 no. 44800 travelled widely in its last years of service. It was still in reasonable condition when this picture was taken at Lostock Hall depot but it may have already reached the end of its working life as it was condemned in the same month.

17.3.68

With the shunter's pole lying just above the engine's buffer beam, 'Jinty' no. 47373, pictured at Workington, presented a scene that was familiar in a great many goods yards. No. 47373 was withdrawn in December 1966, completing just over forty years' service.

9.63

Class 4F 0–6–0 no. 44156 was withdrawn in February 1964 and was photographed at Kettering shed eight months later. Withdrawn engines were often left in shed yards for months at this time until towed away for scrap.

11.10.64

Enthusiasts of all ages crowd the platforms at Blackburn as Class 5 no. 45407 waits to double-head an RCTS 'special' with Standard Class 5 no. 73069. The tender on no. 45407 had a coating of grime which someone had made more apparent by partially rubbing some off. This engine is one of the lucky survivors, and in preservation it works many 'specials'.

4.8.68

One can only guess at how many photographs were taken of the last steam specials. Numerous photographers can be seen in this picture of Standard Class 5 no. 73069, in good external condition, and Class 5 no. 45407 as they run round at Hellifield before working the RCTS 'End of Steam Tour'.

4.8.68

The numerous specials which ran in the last few weeks of steam operation attracted huge crowds. This was the case at Manchester Victoria with 8F no. 48476 and Standard Class 5 no. 73069 heading the RCTS 'End of Steam Tour'.

4.8.68

The sturdy front end of 'Crab' 2–6–0 no. 42776 at Skipton shows signs of damage to the running plate just behind the buffer beam. These engines with their 5MT power classification were very useful for both passenger and freight duties.

9.63

Although steam in BR service had five more months to run, Ivatt 2MT no. 46441 in red livery had already been preserved and was to be seen at Carnforth carrying the number 6441. No. 46441 was in fact completed well into BR days.

17.3.68

(*Opposite top*) There was no regular pattern as to how locomotives were cut up – it seemed to depend on the individuals concerned. Fairburn 2–6–4T no. 42233, at Cohens of Kettering, had already lost most of one side of the cab and bunker, work being concentrated on the boiler.

16.4.67

(*Opposite bottom*) At times the sidings at Cohens of Kettering contained numerous locomotives awaiting cutting up. Here Fairburn 2–6–4Ts nos 42133 and 42086 wait their turn, together with Class 5s and Standards.

16.4.67

Class 4F no. 44109 was in a sorry state when this picture was taken at Cohens scrapyard, Kettering. Quite a number of these engines ended their days here. Some locomotives were cut up almost on arrival, others remained intact for several weeks.

18.10.64

It was always sad to see once-proud locomotives being cut up. Work had only just started on 8F no. 48514 at Cohens of Kettering. The tender had apparently been disposed of first.

16.4.67

Only one of these Johnson 1F 0–6–0Ts was cut up by Cohens of Kettering. No. 41712 was a survivor with a half cab. Fortunately one example, no. 41708, has survived into preservation.

13.12.64

During the 1960s hundreds of steam locomotives were sold to private scrapyards. Cohens of Kettering cut up engines from London Midland, Eastern, Southern and Western Regions, the largest number coming from the LMR. Here, Ivatt 2MT no. 41326 is barely recognizable.

18.10.64

Most enthusiasts during the 1950s would not have given railway notices a second glance, let alone photograph them. Yet many interesting examples were to be seen, such as this L&Y/LNWR joint line trespass warning sign quoting Acts of 1883 and 1884 with a penalty of forty shillings.

13.5.56